The Miniature Horse

Rachel Damon Criscione

The Rosen Publishing Group's

PowerKids Press™

New York

To Laura Whalen, thanks for teaching me the art of friendship

Published in 2007 by The Rosen Publishing Group, Inc.
29 East 21st Street, New York, NY 10010

First Edition

Editor: Amelie von Zumbusch
Book Design: Ginny Chu

Photo Credits: Cover, title page, pp. 12, 16 © Bob Langrish; pp. 4, 15 © Tom Nebbia/Corbis; p. 7 © Kit Houghton/Corbis; p. 8 © Hulton-Deutsch Collection/Corbis; p. 11 © Erik S. Lesser; p. 19 © Barbara Wright/Animals Animals; p. 20 Pedigree and photo courtesy of Sandy Larkin.

Library of Congress Cataloging-in-Publication Data

Criscione, Rachel Damon.
  The miniature horse / Rachel Damon Criscione.— 1st ed.
      p. cm. — (The library of horses)
  Includes bibliographical references and index.
  ISBN 1-4042-3453-5 (library binding)
  1. Miniature horses. I. Title. II. Series: Criscione, Rachel Damon. Library of horses.
SF293.M56C75 2007
636.1'09—dc22
                                        2005034617

Manufactured in the United States of America

Table of Contents

Some miniature horses, like the one shown here, are smaller than a large dog!

A Horse the Size of A Dog

Miniature horses are horses that are about the size of a large dog. They look exactly like full-size horses in every way except miniature horses are much smaller. There are a number of different **breeds** of miniature horses. The American miniature horse, the Falabella, and the South African miniature horse are just some of these breeds.

Miniature horses are too small for anyone except a very young child to ride. However, they make good pets because they are smart and gentle. Some miniature horses are used as guide horses for people who are blind. These horses are specially trained to go anywhere that their **handler** goes. They can go to restaurants, to shopping malls, and even on airplanes.

Little Horses with a Long History

The first-known miniature horses lived in the 1650s. They belonged to Louis XIV, king of France. The king kept the horses in a zoo of unusual animals at his palace in Versailles, France. No one knows what breed these miniature horses were.

Each breed of miniature horse has different **ancestors**. Over time people **bred** small horses and ponies of many breeds together until they produced today's breeds of miniature horses. For example, the Falabella family of Argentina bred small Thoroughbred horses with Shetland ponies in the early 1900s. The little horses that were born were named Falabellas after the family that bred them. Today's American miniature horse is the result of breeding ponies, Falabellas, and other small horses from around the world.

This miniature horse is a Falabella. There are only a few thousand Falabellas in the world today.

This man is teaching a group of boys how to work with a pit pony in a mine in Yorkshire, England.

Pit Ponies

Some miniature horses were bred from working horses. In the 1800s, horses called pit ponies were bred to work in coal mines in Europe. Pit ponies were useful because they could fit into mine tunnels that were too narrow for larger horses. These little horses were so strong that they could pull coal wagons that weighed more than they did.

In the late 1800s, pit ponies were brought from Europe to work in coal mines in Ohio and Virginia. These pit ponies were different from today's miniature horses. Pit ponies were taller and wider. They had legs that seemed short for their round bodies. As time went by, breeders bred pit ponies with other horses to create today's miniature horse.

Horses That Wear Sneakers

As were their ancestors the pit ponies, some miniature horses are working horses. Guide horses are trained to work with people who are blind. Only very small miniature horses can become guide horses. A guide horse must be less than 26 inches (66 cm) from its **withers** to the ground. A guide horse needs to be this small so that its handlers can comfortably hold the horse's **harness**. Guide horses wear a harness on their shoulders while they are working.

Guide horses are trained to go where their handler tells them to go. Some of the places they go, such as to shopping centers and on **escalators**, have slippery floors. Guide horses sometimes wear sneakers over their smooth hooves to keep from slipping on these surfaces.

Guide horses like this one help people who are blind move about. Don and Janet Burleson of North Carolina were the first people to train horses to be guide animals.

This horse is an example of the refined type of miniature horse. This type of horse is popular for miniature-horse shows.

Stock horse–type miniature horses like the one above have large, heavy heads and strong, round bodies.

Miniature-horse Features

Although there are many breeds of miniature horses, all miniature horses are one of two types. The first is called the stock-horse type. This type of horse looks like the strong, sturdy quarter horses that are used on farms. The second is called the **refined** type. These horses are thinner and sleeker.

Both the refined type and the stock-horse type of miniature horses come in many colors. Some miniature horses are all one color. Others have spots of a second color. All miniature horses have thick, woolly coats to keep them warm in the winter. They lose their winter coats in the spring. This leaves the miniature horses with thin coats that keep them cool all summer. Their warm winter coats grow back in the fall.

Miniature-horse Shows

There are hundreds of miniature-horse shows in the United States every year. However, people do not ride the miniature horses in these shows because these horses are too small. Instead handlers guide the horses around a ring.

Miniature-horse shows are separated into classes. Horses in each class are judged on different skills. In the jumping classes, the horse jumps over fences that are up to 44 inches (112 cm) tall. There are usually from six to eight jumps in each jumping class.

Another class in which the miniature horses **compete** is the halter class. In this class the horses are judged on their beauty and **conformation**. Miniature horses with good conformation have straight legs and level backs.

Miniature-horse shows sometimes have costume classes in which horses and their owners dress up in special clothes called a costume. This miniature horse is competing in the costume class at a horse show in Dallas, Texas.

Miniature horses should eat mostly hay or grass. They need to have clean water to drink, too.

A Horse with a Sweet Tooth

Miniature horses need many of the same things that larger horses do. They should have a grassy place to run and **graze**. However, they do not need acres (hectares) of land as a large horse does. They can live in a large backyard.

As all horses do, miniature horses eat grass and grains. They eat so much grass that some people consider them excellent lawn mowers. In the winter there is no grass. Then miniature horses eat hay. Many people who own miniature horses have found that they have a sweet tooth. This means that the horses like to drink and eat sweet things such as soda and candy. However, these foods can make horses sick. Miniature horses should only be given foods such as apples or carrots for a treat.

Always on the Lookout

Miniature horses are aware of any movement around them. As all horses do, they have excellent eyesight. They can see clearly in almost total darkness. A horse's eyes are on the sides of its head. Each eye moves separately. This allows the horse to see different things with each eye.

Horses use their eyesight to make sure they know what is happening around them. They are especially aware when they are with their foals, or baby horses. Miniature-horse foals can be from 16 to 21 inches (41–53 cm) tall when they are born. Foals can stand on their own just 1 hour after they are born, but their mothers still watch over them closely.

Miniature horses hold their ears up when they are on the lookout. This helps them hear well. Horses have very good senses of hearing and smell, as well as a good sense of sight.

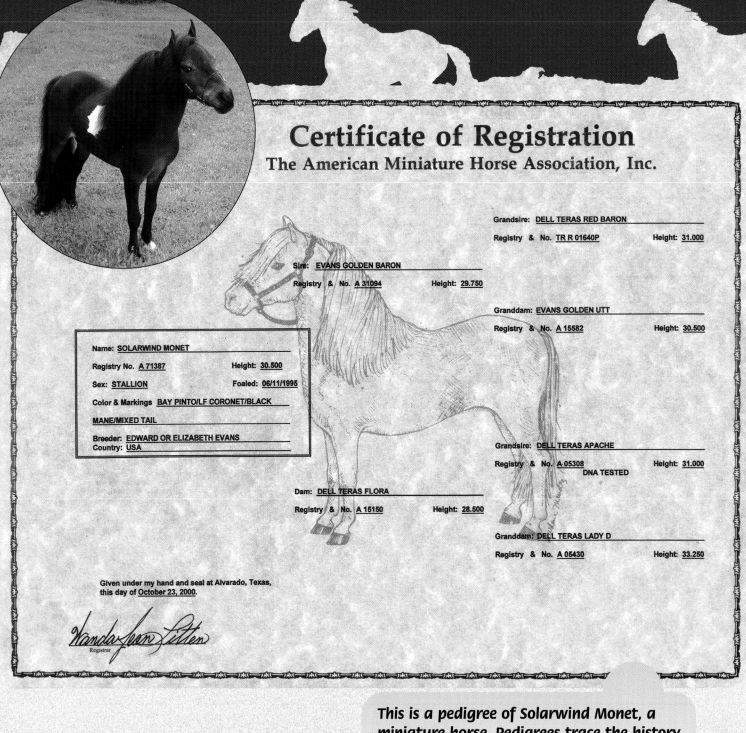

Certificate of Registration
The American Miniature Horse Association, Inc.

Grandsire: DELL TERAS RED BARON

Registry & No. TR R 01640P   Height: 31.000

Sire: EVANS GOLDEN BARON

Registry & No. A 31094   Height: 29.750

Granddam: EVANS GOLDEN UTT

Registry & No. A 15582   Height: 30.500

Name: SOLARWIND MONET

Registry No. A 71387   Height: 30.500

Sex: STALLION   Foaled: 06/11/1995

Color & Markings BAY PINTO/LF CORONET/BLACK

MANE/MIXED TAIL

Breeder: EDWARD OR ELIZABETH EVANS
Country: USA

Grandsire: DELL TERAS APACHE

Registry & No. A 05308   Height: 31.000
                                DNA TESTED

Dam: DELL TERAS FLORA

Registry & No. A 15150   Height: 28.500

Granddam: DELL TERAS LADY D

Registry & No. A 05430   Height: 33.250

Given under my hand and seal at Alvarado, Texas,
this day of October 23, 2000.

Wanda Jean Litten
Registrar

This is a pedigree of Solarwind Monet, a miniature horse. Pedigrees trace the history and bloodlines of an individual horse. The inset shows Solarwind Monet.

The American Miniature Horse Association

One of the first groups formed to honor the miniature horse is the American Miniature Horse Association, or AMHA. It was formed in 1978 when the American miniature horse officially became a breed. The AMHA keeps a **register** of miniature horses. There are more than 160,000 miniature horses registered with the American Miniature Horse Association.

If the distance from the last hair at the base of a horse's mane to the bottom of its hooves is less than 34 inches (86 cm), it may be registered as an American miniature horse. A taller horse cannot be registered with the group, even if its parents are registered American miniature horses. This makes the American miniature horse a **height breed**.

Not Your Average Horse

The miniature horse is a special kind of horse. In some ways they are like full-size horses. Both full-size horses and miniature horses are strong and smart, and they work well with people. However a miniature horse is only about half as tall as a full-size horse.

Miniature horses make wonderful pets for children, older adults, and people with special needs. Many people who are afraid of large horses find that the size and friendly **personality** of the miniature horse make them less fearful. People who do not have enough time or room to keep a large horse often find that they can care for a miniature horse. As the AMHA says, the miniature horse is "the horse for everyone."

Glossary

ancestors (AN-ses-terz) Relatives who lived long ago.

bred (BRED) To have brought a male and a female animal together so they will have babies.

breeds (BREEDZ) Groups of animals that look alike and have the same relatives.

compete (kum-PEET) To oppose another in a game or test.

conformation (kon-for-MAY-shun) The way in which a horse's body is built.

escalators (ES-kuh-lay-terz) Sets of stairs that are always moving up or down.

graze (GRAYZ) To feed on grass.

handler (HAND-ler) Someone in charge of training an animal.

harness (HAR-nes) The leather straps, bands, and other pieces that connect an animal to the people it pulls or leads.

height breed (HYT BREED) A breed that is based only on height.

personality (per-suh-NA-lih-tee) How a person or an animal acts with others.

refined (rih-FYND) Having been made fine, pure, or smooth.

register (REH-jih-ster) An official record book.

withers (WIH-therz) A place between the shoulders of a dog or horse.

Index

Web Sites

Due to the changing nature of Internet links, PowerKids Press has developed an online list of Web sites related to the subject of this book. This site is updated regularly. Please use this link to access the list:
www.powerkidslinks.com/horse/minih/